STEP-by-STEP
SCIENCE

Energy and Movement

Christopher Oxlade

Illustrated by Andrew Farmer, Julia Pearson
and Joanna Williams

W
FRANKLIN WATTS
NEW YORK • LONDON • SYDNEY

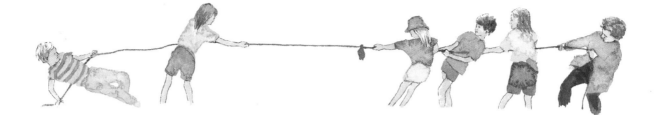

© 1998 Franklin Watts

First published in Great Britain by
Franklin Watts
96 Leonard Street
London
EC2A 4RH

Franklin Watts Australia
14 Mars Road
Lane Cove
NSW 2006
Australia

ISBN: 0 7496 2950 9
10 9 8 7 6 5 4 3 2 1
Dewey Decimal Classification 531
A CIP catalogue record for this book is available from the British Library

Printed in Dubai

Planning and production by Discovery Books Limited
Design: Ian Winton
Editor: Patience Coster

Photographs: Bruce Coleman Limited: page 21 (Geoff Doré); Getty Images:
page 5 (D E Cox), page 6 (Chad Slattery), page 13 (Mark Segal), page 15 (Jeremy Hardie),
page 17 (Jon Nicholson), page 20 (Tony Henshaw), page 22 (Tony Duffy); Robert Harding Picture
Library: page 31 (Pierre Tetrel); NASA: page 26, page 29; Science Photo Library: page 9
(Martin Bond), page 23 (Alex Bartel), page 25 (top, Martin Bond); The Stock Market:
page 10, page 11, page 25 (bottom); Stockfile: cover (Steven Behr).

Contents

Energy for Life

How often do you say, 'I feel tired,' or, 'I haven't got any energy'? Energy lets you do things. It makes your muscles work so that you can walk, run and jump. In fact, nothing would happen without energy.

All living things need energy. Animals eat food to get the energy they need. Big animals need more energy than small animals, so they have to eat more food.

Energy lights and heats our homes. Household gadgets such as televisions and cookers are worked by energy.

Energy makes the working parts of machines go round or up and down. Think of the energy you need to ride your bicycle, especially up a steep hill! Energy is needed to make bicycles, cars, trains and planes move.

Energy Everywhere

Energy comes in many forms. You get energy by eating food which has energy stored in it. Food is the **fuel** that makes our bodies work. The energy in this fuel is called **chemical energy**.

When somebody pushes you on a swing, that person makes you move. Anything that moves has energy. This form of energy is called movement energy. Things spinning round on the spot have movement energy, too.

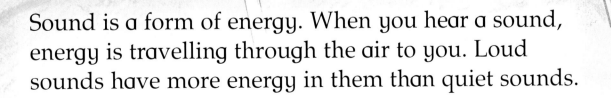

Sound is a form of energy. When you hear a sound, energy is travelling through the air to you. Loud sounds have more energy in them than quiet sounds.

Heat Energy

Heat is another form of energy. Adding heat to an object makes it hotter. Taking heat away makes it colder.

If you put cold hands around a hot mug of milk, your hands warm up because heat moves from the hot drink to your cold hands. Heat energy always tries to move from hot things to colder things.

Heat moves from hot liquid to colder hands and air.

The higher the reading on the thermometer scale, the higher the person's temperature.

Temperature measures how hot or cold something is. You measure temperature in degrees Celsius (°C) or degrees Fahrenheit (°F) with a thermometer.

Making Use of Solar Energy

The solar panels on the roofs of these houses collect the Sun's heat rays. The energy from these rays is used to heat water, which in turn heats the buildings by passing through central heating systems.

Heat can also move around in gases and liquids. When one part of a gas or liquid is warmed up, it floats upwards, carrying the heat energy with it. This is how heat spreads through a pan of water on a cooker.

Inside the pan, warm liquid rises and cooler water sinks down to be heated.

Heat

Changing Energy

When you run, you give yourself movement energy. This comes from energy stored in your body. So you have changed stored energy to movement energy. Energy often changes from one form to another.

This match-head has chemical energy stored in it. When the match is struck, the energy changes into heat and light.

As you climb to the top of a slide you are giving yourself a type of energy called **potential energy**.

When you begin to slide down, potential energy is changed into movement energy.

WHIZ-THUD!

1 Stand with a thick magazine in your hand, level with your waist.

2 Drop the magazine to the floor.

3 As you lift the magazine, you give it potential energy. As the magazine falls, the potential energy changes to movement energy. But what happens to the energy when the book hits the floor? It turns into sound energy that you hear as a thud.

When you rub your hands together they warm up. The rubbing movement changes movement energy into heat energy.

Gas is a fuel which makes heat energy when it burns. Burning gas is used to make these hot-air balloons fly.

Energy at Home

We rely on energy in our homes every hour of every day. We need electrical energy to make lights work and heat energy for cooking. In the winter, we need more heat energy for keeping warm. We also need electrical energy to make gadgets, such as televisions and computers, work.

People sometimes use gas for heating and cooking. The gas comes into their homes along a pipe. Gas is a good fuel. It burns very well, giving out plenty of heat. Coal and oil are fuels, too.

Moving Around

A **battery** is a store of electrical energy. Batteries are useful because they allow us to carry electrical gadgets.

People sometimes burn wood to make heat energy for cooking and keeping warm.

Where Energy Comes From

Electricity is very convenient to use. You simply push a plug into the wall and turn on. But where does electricity come from? And where do fuels such as coal and gas come from?

Gas is **extracted** from rocks deep under the ground. It is **processed** and then carried to our houses along a pipeline.

Hydro-electric dams use the energy in flowing water to make electricity.

Coal is also found underground. Miners dig it out and transport it to the surface. Coal is a fossil fuel. It is made from dead plants which were buried underground millions of years ago.

The wind blows these **wind turbines** around. The turbines turn machines called **generators**, which make electricity.

Oil Rigs at Sea

Pipes from this oil rig reach down into the sea bed where the oil is trapped under layers of rock. The oil is pumped up the pipes to the surface.

Electricity is made in huge power stations by burning coal, gas or oil. It travels from the power station to your home along thick cables.

Sometimes power stations are built across **estuaries**. They use the movement of the tides to make electricity.

15

Forces

When you push or pull on something you make what is called a force. Can you think of the forces you need to ride your bicycle? To make the bicycle move, you push down on the pedals with your feet. This push is a force. To slow down, you pull on the brake levers. This pull is a force, too.

A force has two parts. The first part is its size and the second part is the direction in which it pushes or pulls. On your bicycle, you press down on the pedals, so the direction of the force is down. You pull back on the brake levers.

Often there are two or more forces, pushing or pulling on an object. Sometimes they push in the same direction. Sometimes they push in different directions. The wind pushes on this windsurfer's sail. She pulls on the sail to keep it upright.

Balanced Forces

In this tug-of-war, each team pulls on the rope in the opposite direction. The teams in the first picture are pulling with the same amount of force, so the two forces are balanced and the rope stays still.

If one team pulls with more force than the other team, the two sides will become unbalanced. The rope will move and the teams may fall over.

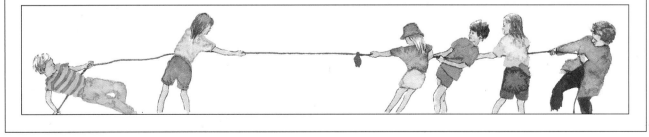

What Do Forces Do?

What happens when you push yourself along on skates? You begin to move. You always need a force to make something start moving. If you didn't push yourself along, you and the skates would stay still.

Forces can do many things. They can tear things.

Forces can squash and stretch things. When you sit on a bouncy toy, your body pushes down on it. The toy cannot move downwards because of the ground underneath, so it gets squashed instead.

Forces can make things turn round.
To turn a steering wheel, you push
on one side and pull on the other.

Pushing
and pulling
twist the
top off a
bottle.

Forces can bend
things.

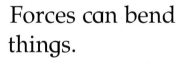

Speeding Along

How fast can you walk? If you were to walk non-stop for an hour, you would probably cover about four kilometres. You would have walked at four kilometres per hour. This measurement is called your speed. Sprinters can run at about thirty-six kilometres per hour, but only for a short distance before they get tired!

Some things go very fast. A jet aircraft zooms through the air at nearly 1,000 kilometres an hour.

Some things go very slowly. Snails slither along at about ten metres an hour.

As Fast as Light

Light rays move very fast indeed. They travel at 300,000 kilometres per second! The Sun is about 150 million kilometres away from Earth, but light from it reaches us in just eight minutes!

Faster and Slower

Things don't travel at the same speed all the time. They sometimes speed up, or go faster. They sometimes slow down, or go slower. Things don't speed up or slow down on their own. They need a force to make them do it.

Speeding up is called acceleration. The driver of this racing car presses down on the accelerator pedal to make the car accelerate along the track. The force making the car accelerate comes from its engine.

Free-Fall

Sky-divers fall quickly through the air for thousands of metres before opening their parachutes. They open their parachutes to slow themselves down before they hit the ground.

Slowing down is called deceleration. As she enters the water, this diver decelerates. The **drag** of the water slows her down.

Light and Heavy

Why is it easier to move a sledge with one person on it than it is to move a sledge with two people on it? The answer is that the second sledge is heavier. It takes more force to move a heavy thing than a light thing.

Bigger forces have more effect than smaller forces. So if two people push a sledge, it speeds up more quickly than if one person pushes it.

A railway locomotive makes a huge pull to start hundreds of heavy trucks moving. The trucks only move very slowly to begin with.

A tiny grasshopper only makes a small push with its legs, but because it is so light, it can jump very high and very quickly.

Gravity

Have you ever heard the saying 'What goes up must come down'? When you jump in the air, you always fall back to the ground. The force that pulls you down is called gravity. Gravity pulls everything on Earth downwards.

Gravity on the Moon

The force of gravity is much less on the Moon than on Earth. This is because the Moon is smaller. It is easy to jump high on the Moon because there is less gravity. In the depths of space, far from the Earth and Moon, there is no gravity. In deep space an **astronaut** would feel weightless.

This picture shows some of the ways in which gravity affects people and things. The weighing scales measure the extent to which gravity pulls a person downwards. This pull is called 'weight'. Weight pulls the rollercoaster down the track and the boat down the water-slide.

Making Circles

How many things can you think of that move round and round in a circle? Wheels? Roundabouts? The sails of a windmill?

When things move in a circle, they have to keep changing direction to keep going round. A force is needed to change direction. The force is called centripetal force. It always points into the middle of the circle.

This space station is moving around the Earth in a huge circle called an orbit. The centripetal force that keeps it travelling in orbit is gravity. If there was no gravity, the space station would fly off into space.

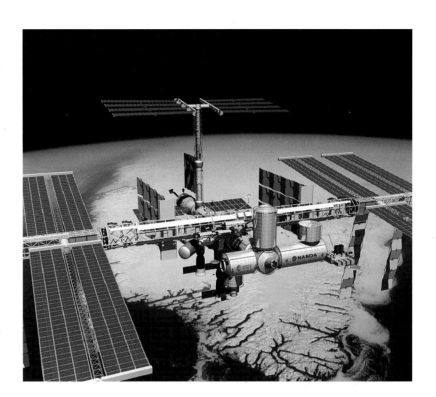

CORK ON A STRING

1 Tie a piece of string about 1 metre long around the middle of a cork.

2 Swing the cork slowly around on the string. Make sure that the cork doesn't hit anybody or knock anything over. You need to pull on the string to keep the cork moving round its circle.

3 What happens if you let go of the string?

Machines

Machines are things that help us to do jobs. When you think of a machine, you might think of a digger on a building site, a vacuum cleaner or a washing machine in your kitchen. But some machines are much simpler than these. A tin-opener and a pair of scissors are machines, too.

A pulley is a wheel with a groove around the rim for carrying a rope. A small pull down on the rope makes a large pull up on the bucket. Without the pulley, the bucket would be too heavy to lift.

A lever is a very simple machine. These people are using levers to move a heavy pipe. A small push down on the long arm of the lever makes a large push up on the pipe.

Raising Water

This machine is called an Archimedean screw. When the person turns the handle, the screw scoops up water at the bottom end and pours it out at the top end.

These machines on a building site have powerful engines which move their parts. They can lift and move very heavy objects.

Glossary

Astronaut: A person whose job it is to explore outer space

Battery: An object which stores electricity

Chemical energy: A form of energy which is stored inside substances. Plants, humans and batteries all contain substances that store chemical energy

Drag: A force that slows down an object's movement

Estuary: A wide river mouth

Extracted: Taken out

Fuel: Any material, such as coal, oil, gas or wood, burned to give heat or power

Generator: A machine that changes mechanical energy into electrical energy

Hydro-electric dam: A dam used to make electricity from water power

Potential energy: The energy a body has because of the position it is in

Processed: Prepared by a special treatment, or process

Solar energy: Energy from the Sun

Wind turbine: A propeller-like machine which is driven round by the wind

Index